HOW TO DRAW COMICS

BY GWENN MERCADOOCASIO

LONGMEADOW
PRESS

HOW TO DRAW COMICS

BY GWENN MERCADOOCASIO

COLORED AND LETTERED BY
CLIFF VANMETER AND JENNI BARLOW

Published by Longmeadow Press, 201 High Ridge Road, Stamford, CT 06904.

ISBN: 0-681-00424-X

Printed in United States

First Longmeadow Press Edition

0 9 8 7 6 5 4 3 2 1

THIS BOOK IS DEDICATED TO
MY POP, **PHIL SEULING**,
WHO GAVE ME MY FIRST BOX OF COMIC BOOKS.

WITH THANKS FOR ALL THE LOVE AND
SUPPORT TO MY HUSBAND **HARVO**,
AUNT BOBBIE, MY **MOM**, AND "**ESTER**".

P.S. TO ALL MY STUDENTS:
THANKS, AND **KEEP DRAWING!**

INTRODUCTION

COMIC BOOKS ARE AN ORIGINAL AMERICAN ART FORM, AND EVEN THOUGH THEY HAVE A LOT IN COMMON WITH BOOKS AND MOVIES, THEY ARE **UNIQUE**.

IN A COMIC BOOK THE RELATIONSHIP BETWEEN THE WORDS AND PICTURES COMBINE TO TELL A STORY. THE PICTURES **SHOW** US ONE PART OF THE STORY WHILE THE WORDS **TELL** US ANOTHER, IN THIS WAY WE ARE GIVEN ALL OF THE INFORMATION THE ARTIST AND WRITER WANT US TO HAVE. THE WORDS AND PICTURES **SUPPORT** EACH OTHER.

A COMIC BOOK CAN BE DRAWN IN ANY STYLE, YOU HAVE YOUR OWN WAY OF LOOKING AT THINGS, AND YOUR OWN WAY OF PUTTING THOSE THINGS DOWN ON PAPER - YOUR OWN **STYLE**. WHILE YOU CAN LEARN A LOT BY IMITATING OTHER ARTISTS, YOUR WAY OF DRAWING COMICS WILL BE THE MOST INTERESTING IN THE LONG RUN, SO DEVELOP IT!

IT TAKES A LOT OF WORK TO MAKE COMICS, BUT IT CAN ALSO BE A LOT OF FUN! IT'S A GREAT FEELING WHEN YOU CAN INTEREST SOMEONE IN SPENDING TIME IN A WORLD YOU'VE CREATED. IF YOU CAN THRILL THEM OR MAKE THEM LAUGH WHILE THEY'RE IN THAT WORLD, THEN IT'S JUST THAT MUCH BETTER A FEELING! REMEMBER, IT TAKES PATIENCE, PRACTICE, AND A LOT OF TIME TO MAKE COMICS. PUT THE TIME IN AND YOU'LL GET THE RESULTS YOU WANT.

THE INFORMATION IN THIS BOOK IS GIVEN TO YOU IN FOUR CHAPTERS. EACH CHAPTER DEALS WITH A DIFFERENT ASPECT OF DRAWING AND CREATING COMICS. AT THE END OF THIS BOOK YOU WILL FIND A LIST OF EXERCISES THAT WILL HELP TO IMPROVE YOUR SKILLS.

HAVE FUN!

MEASURING THE COMICS PAGE

STANDARD COMIC PAGES ARE ELEVEN INCHES BY SEVENTEEN INCHES, WITH AN IMAGE SIZE OF TEN INCHES BY FIFTEEN INCHES. THE **IMAGE SIZE** IS THE AREA OF THE PAPER ACTUALLY USED FOR THE COMIC ART. THERE IS A HALF INCH LEFT ON EACH SIDE, AND AN INCH AT THE TOP AND BOTTOM FOR THE BORDER. THIS BORDER IS CALLED THE **"GRIP"** AND IS LEFT THERE FOR THE PRINTER SO THAT THE ARTWORK MAY BE HANDLED WITHOUT DIRTYING IT.

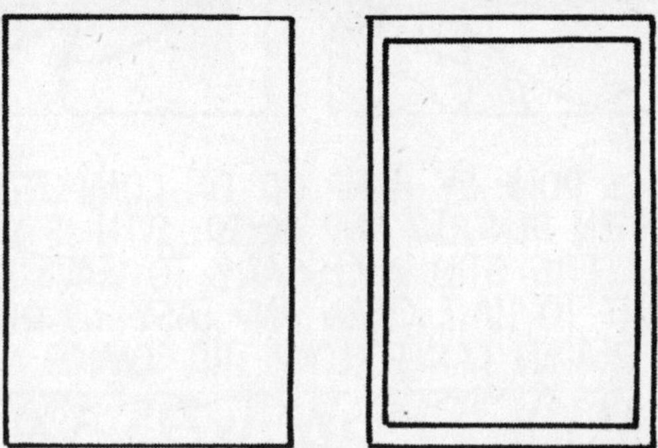

THE PAGES ARE **REDUCED** TO APPROXIMATELY SIXTY PERCENT OF THEIR ORIGINAL SIZE WHEN THEY ARE READY TO BE PRINTED AS COMIC BOOKS.

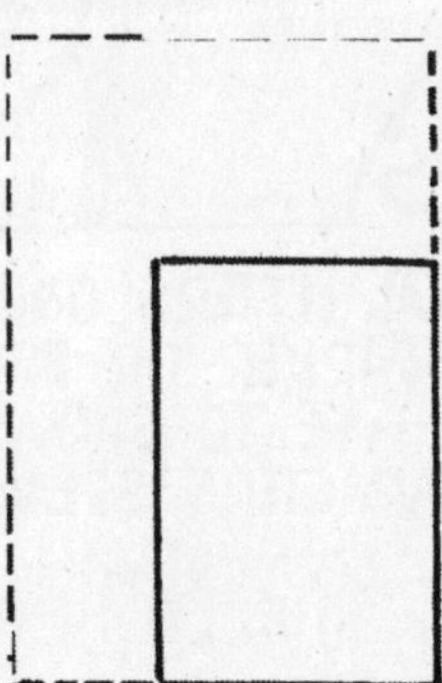

THE AVERAGE SIZE OF A FINISHED COMIC BOOK IS TEN AND ONE QUARTER INCHES BY SIX AND FIVE EIGHTHS OF AN INCH.

GUTTERS ARE THE SPACES BETWEEN THE PANELS ON A COMIC PAGE. BEFORE A COMICS PAGE IS REDUCED, THE GUTTERS SHOULD BE ONE QUARTER INCH. IT'S IMPORTANT TO KEEP THE GUTTERS UNIFORM, UNLESS YOU HAVE GOOD REASON NOT TO, SINCE IT MAKES THE COMIC PAGE EASIER AND "CLEANER" TO READ.

LETTERING FOR COMICS IS DONE BY HAND OR ON COMPUTERS AND IS ADDED AFTER THE COMIC PAGE HAS BEEN PENCILED AND INKED. EVEN IF YOU NEVER PLAN TO DO YOUR OWN LETTERING, IT IS STILL NECESSARY TO LEAVE ROOM FOR IT IN YOUR PANELS, IT'S IMPORTANT TO HAVE CLEAN AND EASY TO READ LETTERING SO THAT YOUR READER CAN FOLLOW THE COMICS STORY!

COMICS ARE WRITTEN IN CAPITAL LETTERS ONLY. WHEN A WORD IS VERY IMPORTANT, OR LOUD IT IS MADE DARKER OR **BOLDER** THAN THE REST. YOU CAN ALSO USE DIFFERENT KINDS OF TYPE TO SHOW THE DIFFERENT WAYS YOUR CHARACTERS SPEAK.

A ROBOT MIGHT SPEAK LIKE THIS: HELLO HUMAN. WHAT DO YOU WANT?

WHEN LETTERING BY HAND IT IS EASIEST TO USE A LETTERING GUIDE SET AT THREE AND ONE HALF. IF YOU DON'T HAVE A LETTERING GUIDE, MEASURE CAREFULLY ONE EIGHTH OF AN INCH LINES FOR THE LETTERS AND ONE SIXTEENTH OF AN INCH SPACES BETWEEN THE LINES OF LETTERING.

BELOW ARE TWO TYPES OF LETTERING USED IN COMICS. ON THE LEFT IS A COMPUTER TYPE CALLED **WHIZ BANG**. ON THE RIGHT IS A HAND LETTERED ALPHABET. USE THESE TO PRACTICE YOUR OWN LETTERING SKILLS.

A B C D E F G H I J K L M
N O P Q R S T U V W X Y Z
1 2 3 4 5 6 7 8 9 0
! ?

A B C D E F G H I J K L M
N O P Q R S T U V W X Y Z
1 2 3 4 5 6 7 8 9 10
! ?

THE LETTERING YOU USE FOR THE TITLE OF YOUR COMICS AS WELL AS THE "HEADER" ON THE COVER OF THE COMIC BOOK SHOULD TELL YOUR AUDIENCE SOMETHING ABOUT THE STORY ITSELF. **SHADOWSTARS** IS A COMBINATION OF THE TWO CHARACTER'S NAMES, AND THE LETTERING IS BOLD AND FUTURISTIC LOOKING. THE TITLE OF THE STORY, "FOUR'S COMPANY, FIVE'S A CROWD", IS A KIND OF CARNIVAL LETTERING, CHOSEN BECAUSE THE STORY TAKES PLACE IN AN AMUSEMENT PARK.

IF YOU SPEND TIME CHOOSING THE BEST LETTERING FOR YOUR STORY IT WILL PAY OFF SINCE IT WILL ONLY MAKE YOUR STORY THAT MUCH BETTER TO LOOK AT OVERALL!

PANELS

THE PICTURES IN COMICS ARE GENERALLY DRAWN INSIDE BOXES CALLED **PANELS**. YOU MAY USE AS MANY PANELS ON EACH PAGE AS YOU NEED TO TELL A STORY, BUT AS A GENERAL RULE NO MORE THAN SIX PANELS PER PAGE IS BEST.

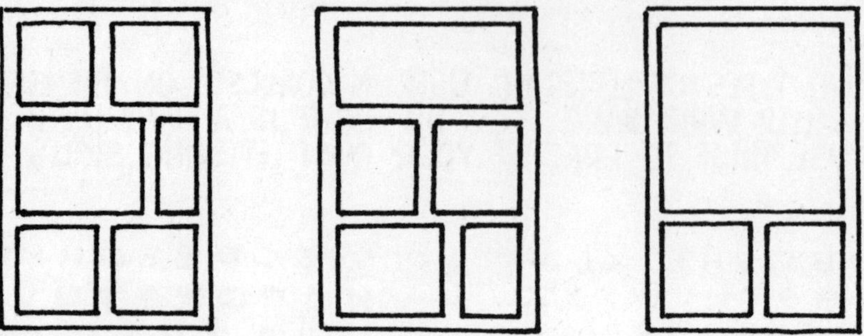

PANELS CAN BE ANY SIZE OR SHAPE AT ALL. IT IS A GOOD IDEA TO SKETCH YOUR PICTURES AND WORDS IN AND THEN RULE YOUR PANELS AROUND THEM SO YOU'LL KNOW HOW LARGE YOU'LL NEED YOUR PANELS TO BE.

YOUR PANELS SHOULD BE LARGE ENOUGH TO SHOW THE INFORMATION YOU WANT IN THEM CLEARLY WITHOUT SQUEEZING THE PICTURES OR WORDS. A WELL DRAWN COMIC CAN END UP LOOKING TERRIBLE IF THE WORDS ARE SQUEEZED IN AS AN AFTERTHOUGHT, SO BE VERY CAREFUL TO ALLOW ENOUGH ROOM FOR THEM!

THERE ARE MANY **TYPES OF PANELS**. THE LARGEST IS ACTUALLY CALLED A **SPLASH- PAGE**, AND IS AN ENTIRE PAGE OF A COMIC BOOK! SPLASH PAGES ARE MOST OFTEN USED AT THE BEGINNING OF A COMIC TO SHOW THE AUDIENCE AS MUCH INFORMATION AS POSSIBLE. WHEN SPLASH-PAGES ARE USED IN OTHER PARTS OF A COMIC THEY ARE USUALLY TO EMPHASIZE ACTION SCENES.

A **SPLASH-PANEL** IS ANY PANEL THAT IS HALF A COMIC PAGE OR LARGER. A SPLASH-PANEL IS USED IN THE SAME WAY AS A SPLASH-PAGE, OR WHEN A SMALLER PANEL WOULDN'T ALLOW ENOUGH SPACE TO SHOW ALL OF THE INFORMATION NEEDED. IN THE BONUS COMIC, **SHADOWSTARS**, THERE ARE TWO SPLASH-PANELS ON THE FIRST PAGE. THESE HELP TO ESTABLISH THE LOCATION OF THE STORY FOR THE AUDIENCE.

A **VIGNETTE** IS AN IMAGE OR IMAGES THAT ARE NOT FRAMED BY A PANEL. VIGNETTES ARE A NICE WAY TO BREAK FROM THE STORY FOR A CHANGE OF PACE, OR TO DRAW SPECIAL ATTENTION TO WHAT IS TAKING PLACE IN THE VIGNETTE. IN **SHADOWSTARS**, THE FIRST PANEL ON PAGE THREE IS A VIGNETTE. THE VIGNETTE WAS USED HERE TO DRAW ATTENTION TO THE CHARACTERS AS THEY CHANGE INTO THEIR SUPERHERO ALTER-EGOS.

BY CHANGING THE SIZE OF YOUR PANELS YOU CAN CHANGE THE WAY THE AUDIENCE WILL READ THE INFORMATION IN THEM. WHEN ALL OF YOUR PANELS ARE THE SAME SIZE, THE INFORMATION IN THEM WILL SEEM TO HAVE EQUAL IMPORTANCE. LOOK AT THE TWO EXAMPLES BELOW. THINK ABOUT WHICH PANEL SEEMS TO DRAW YOUR ATTENTION IN EACH OF THEM, AND WHY THAT PANEL DOES DRAW YOUR ATTENTION.

YOU CAN ALSO CHANGE TIME BY CHANGING YOUR PANELS. THE SAME INFORMATION SHOWN IN PANELS OF DIFFERENT SIZES CAN SEEM TO SLOW DOWN OR SPEED UP THE ACTION IN THE PANELS. LOOK AT THE EXAMPLES BELOW. THINK ABOUT WHICH PANELS SEEM TO BE FASTER OR SLOWER THAN THE OTHERS AND WHY THEY SEEM THAT WAY.

WORDS IN COMICS

WORDS IN COMICS ARE WRITTEN FOUR WAYS: IN **BALLOONS**, IN **THOUGHT BALLOONS**, IN **CAPTIONS**, AND AS **SOUND EFFECTS**.

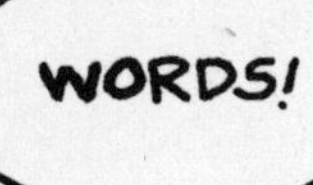

YES, WORDS.

WORDS IN **BALLOONS** ARE THE DIALOGUE, THE WORDS SPOKEN BY YOUR CHARACTERS.

NO KIDDING! REALLY?

WORDS IN **THOUGHT BALLOONS** ARE THE WORDS YOUR CHARACTERS THINK TO THEMSELVES, AND DON'T SPEAK ALOUD.

WORDS IN **CAPTIONS** ARE THE NARRATIVE PART OF YOUR COMICS STORY. THESE ARE USED TO EXPLAIN SOMETHING TO YOUR AUDIENCE THAT IS NOT POSSIBLE TO SHOW OR HAVE YOUR CHARACTERS SAY OR THINK. BE CAREFUL NOT TO USE TOO MANY CAPTIONS. THEY SLOW YOUR AUDIENCE DOWN AND CAN MAKE A STORY DULL.

SOUND EFFECTS ARE THE NOISES MADE BY THE PEOPLE OR THINGS IN YOUR COMIC BOOK. A WHISTLING TEAPOT, A SLAMMING DOOR, OR A SUPERHERO FLYING OFF ARE ALL PICTURES THAT COULD USE SOUND EFFECTS.

THE LETTERING IN SOUND EFFECTS CAN VARY TO SHOW BETTER WHAT KIND OF NOISE THE SOUND EFFECT IS. LOOK AT THE DIFFERENT STYLES OF LETTERING IN THE SOUND EFFECTS EXAMPLES ABOVE. IT WOULD NOT HAVE WORKED AS WELL IF THE LETTERING FOR THE TEAPOT'S WHISTLE WAS THE SAME AS THE LETTERING USED FOR THE SLAMMING DOOR.

ZOOM!

POW!

WHISTLE

CAMERA ANGLES

WHETHER YOU WRITE YOUR COMICS STORY OR DRAW A STORY THAT SOMEONE ELSE HAS WRITTEN, YOU WILL NEED TO KNOW HOW TO TELL A STORY IN A COMIC BOOK.

DON'T GET NERVOUS!

AS YOU FIRST LOOK THROUGH THE LIST OF TECHNIQUES FOR STORYTELLING, IT MAY SEEM LIKE THERE IS AN AWFUL LOT TO REMEMBER. CHANCES ARE YOU ARE ALREADY FAMILIAR WITH A LOT OF THESE IF YOU HAVE EVER WATCHED T.V. OR SEEN A MOVIE. AS YOU PRACTICE AND IMPROVE YOUR SKILLS THESE TECHNIQUES WILL BECOME SO NATURAL TO YOU THAT YOU WILL NOT BE AWARE THAT YOU ARE USING THEM!

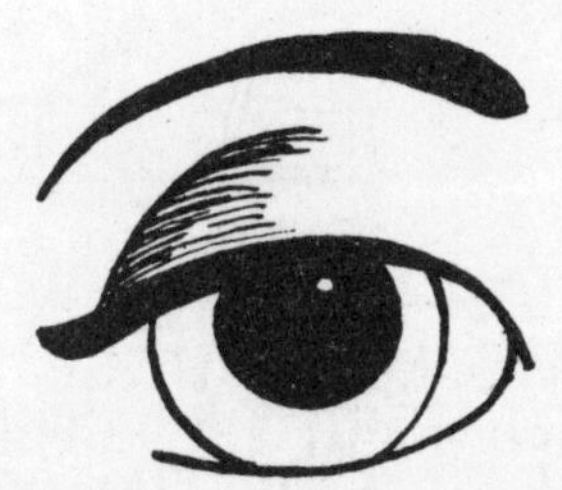

THE **CAMERA ANGLE** IS WHAT TELLS THE AUDIENCE WHERE THEY ARE IN RELATION TO THE IMAGES ON YOUR COMICS PAGE. WITH CERTAIN ANGLES YOU CAN MAKE YOUR AUDIENCE LOOK UP OR DOWN AT THE IMAGES YOU HAVE DRAWN. IN A WAY, THE CAMERA ANGLE BECOMES THE AUDIENCE'S "EYES".

THE WAY YOU SEE AN IMAGE CAN CHANGE THE WAY YOU FEEL ABOUT IT. MOST PEOPLE FEEL AWE-STRUCK LOOKING UP AT THE WORLD TRADE CENTER, AND SUPERIOR TO THE "LITTLE PEOPLE" RUNNING AROUND BELOW THEM WHEN THEY LOOK DOWN FROM THE TOP OF IT.

BY CHANGING YOUR CAMERA ANGLES YOU CAN CHANGE THE WAY YOUR AUDIENCE FEELS FROM ONE PANEL TO THE NEXT. AT THE SAME TIME, BY KEEPING YOUR CAMERA ANGLE THE SAME THROUGHOUT YOUR STORY, YOU LEAD YOUR AUDIENCE TO EXPECT MORE OF THE SAME. WHEN YOU DO CHANGE CAMERA ANGLES IT WILL CREATE A GREAT SURPRISE IN YOUR AUDIENCE.

THE **CLOSE-UP** IS A CAMERA ANGLE THAT BRINGS THE IMAGE SO NEAR TO THE AUDIENCE THAT IT FILLS THE PANEL. THIS GIVES THE AUDIENCE A CHANCE TO EXAMINE THE IMAGE CAREFULLY, AND ESTABLISHES A SENSE OF INTIMACY. IT CAN MAGNIFY AN EMOTION. THE CLOSE-UP OF **TOXIN** ON PAGE THREE OF **SHADOWSTARS** SHOWS THE AUDIENCE JUST HOW CRAZY THE CHARACTER IS!

THE **EXTREME CLOSE-UP** ZEROS IN ON ONE PART OF THE IMAGE, MAKING IT "LARGER THAN LIFE" AND VERY IMPORTANT TO THE AUDIENCE. EXTREME CLOSE-UPS CAN MAKE THE AUDIENCE UNCOMFORTABLE BECAUSE THE IMAGE IS SO CLOSE. IT'S NOT A NATURAL WAY OF LOOKING AT THINGS, BUT IT'S USEFUL FOR SHOWING STRONG EMOTIONS, OR TO CREATE CONFUSION IN YOUR AUDIENCE.

A **MEDIUM-SHOT** IS PROBABLY THE MOST COMMON AND THE MOST COMFORTABLE FOR YOUR AUDIENCE. WHILE IT MAY NOT BE A COMPLETE IMAGE, IT SETS THE IMAGE AT A NATURAL DISTANCE FROM YOUR AUDIENCE, MAKING IT ACCESSIBLE, NOT THREATENING. USE MEDIUM SHOTS TO GIVE GENERAL INFORMATION AND TO KEEP YOUR STORY MOVING ALONG.

THE **LONG-SHOT** ALLOWS THE AUDIENCE TO SEE A COMPLETE IMAGE AND HAS MORE INFORMATION IN THE PANEL. IT SEPARATES THE AUDIENCE FROM THE IMAGE, BUT IS VERY USEFUL FOR SHOWING ACTION SCENES. THE TWO LARGE PANELS ON PAGE ONE OF **SHADOWSTAR** ARE LONG-SHOTS. THE **EXTREME LONG-SHOT** IS USED MOST FOR ESTABLISHING LOCATIONS, OR TO GIVE THE AUDIENCE AS MUCH INFORMATION AS IS POSSIBLE. THE FIRST PANEL ON PAGE TWO OF **SHADOWSTAR** IS AN EXTREME LONG-SHOT.

THE **WORM'S-EYE VIEW** PLACES THE AUDIENCE BELOW THE IMAGE IN THE PANEL, SO THAT THEY ARE FORCED TO LOOK UP TO IT. THIS CAN MAKE THE IMAGE SEEM MENACING. PANEL THREE, PAGE THREE OF **SHADOWSTARS** IS A WORM'S-EYE VIEW.

THE **BIRD'S-EYE VIEW**, OR **OVERHEAD SHOT** FORCES THE AUDIENCE TO LOOK DOWN ON THE IMAGE IN THE PANEL. THIS MAKES THE IMAGE SEEM SMALLER, LESS IMPORTANT, OR EVEN VULNERABLE TO THE AUDIENCE.ON PAGE FOUR OF **SHADOWSTARS**, PANEL TWO IS AN OVERHEAD SHOT.

AN **OBLIQUE ANGLE** IS ONE WHERE THE IMAGE IN THE PANEL APPEARS SKEWED, OR TILTED BECAUSE OF THE WAY THE AUDIENCE IS BEING MADE TO LOOK AT IT. THIS MAKES THE IMAGE IN THE PANEL SEEM STRANGE ITSELF AND IT ALERTS THE AUDIENCE THAT SOMETHING IS NOT RIGHT. PANEL ONE ON PAGE FOUR OF **SHADOWSTARS** IS AN OBLIQUE ANGLE.

THERE ARE MANY VARIATIONS ON THE ANGLES MENTIONED HERE. ANY ANGLE CAN BE MADE EXTREME, OR CAN BE COMBINED WITH ANOTHER ANGLE. USING CAMERA ANGLES WILL ENABLE YOU TO MANIPULATE YOUR AUDIENCE'S VIEWPOINT AND TELL A MORE POWERFUL STORY.

COMPOSITION

THE WAY THAT THE INFORMATION IN A PANEL IS PUT TOGETHER IS CALLED THE **COMPOSITION** OF THE PANEL. AMERICANS READ FROM LEFT TO RIGHT, TOP TO BOTTOM. EVEN THOUGH YOUR AUDIENCE SEES A PANEL AS A WHOLE, THE INFORMATION IN THE PANEL IS STILL READ FROM LEFT TO RIGHT, THEN TOP TO BOTTOM.

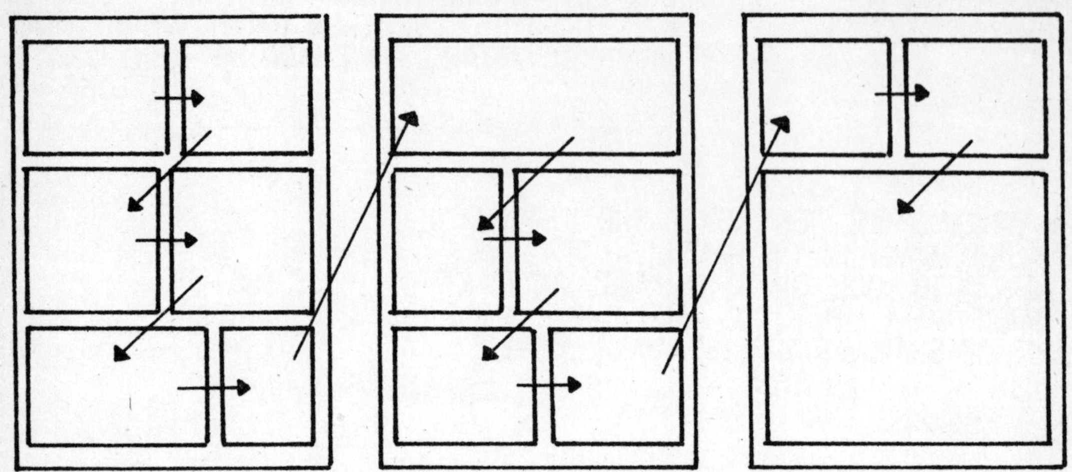

IN EVERY PANEL THERE IS A CERTAIN BALANCE, AND BY PLAYING WITH THE COMPOSITION OF THE PANEL, YOU CAN CHANGE THE BALANCE IN A PANEL AND DIRECT YOUR AUDIENCE'S ATTENTION WHERE YOU WANT IT. LOOK AT THE THREE PANELS BELOW:

THE INFORMATION IN THE FIRST PANEL IS BALANCED. THE BALL IS CENTERED, AND EVERYTHING SEEMS TO BE IN ORDER. IN THE SECOND PANEL, THE BALL IS DOWN IN THE BOTTOM-RIGHT CORNER. WHY? WE EXPECT INFORMATION TO BE GIVEN TO US IN A CERTAIN ORDER. THIS IMAGE IS DISTURBING, SINCE IT SEEMS THAT THE INFORMATION IN THE BEGINNING OF THE PANEL IS MISSING. IN THE THIRD PANEL, THE BALL IS IN THE UPPER-LEFT CORNER. THE EMPTY SPACE IN THE REST OF THE PANEL LEADS US TO BELIEVE THAT MORE IS YET TO COME, AND SETS UP A SENSE OF EXPECTATION IN THE AUDIENCE.

CONTINUITY AND FORESHADOWING

WHEN YOU ARE TELLING A STORY WITH PICTURES YOU HAVE TO BE CAREFUL TO KEEP THE IMAGES IN YOUR STORY CONSISTANT. IF A CHARACTER IS WALKING ALONG HOLDING AN UMBRELLA, THEN THAT CHARACTER CAN'T HAVE THE UMBRELLA IN PANELS ONE AND THREE WITHOUT HAVING IT IN PANEL TWO ALSO. WHEN THE ACTION IN YOUR PANELS IS TAKING PLACE IN THE SAME LOCATION, THE BACKGROUNDS MUST BE CONSISTANT TOO. THIS IS CALLED **CONTINUITY**. IT KEEPS YOUR STORY MOVING ALONG, AND HELPS THE AUDIENCE TO BETTER FOLLOW YOUR CHARACTER'S ACTIONS.

SURPRISES CAN MAKE A STORY MORE INTERESTING, BUT YOUR AUDIENCE NEEDS TO HAVE SOME REASON TO BELIEVE THAT THEY ARE POSSIBLE WHEN THE SURPRISES TAKE PLACE. IF A THREE YEAR OLD CHILD IS SUDDENLY SHOWN DRIVING A CAR, YOUR AUDIENCE IS GOING TO WANT TO KNOW HOW THAT CHILD MANAGED TO DO IT!

IF, EARLIER IN YOUR STORY, THE AUDIENCE WAS SHOWN THAT THE CHILD LOVED CARS, OR HAD A COLLECTION OF MODEL CARS, OR HAD POSSIBLY STUDIED SOMEONE WHO WAS DRIVING A CAR, THEN IT WOULD BE BELIEVABLE. SETTING INFORMATION UP LIKE THIS FOR YOUR AUDIENCE IS CALLED **FORESHADOWING**.

THUMBNAIL TO FINISH

ONCE YOU HAVE A STORY YOU'D LIKE TO DRAW AS A COMIC BOOK YOU NEED TO FIND OUT HOW MANY PAGES IT WILL TAKE TO TELL IT IN. COMIC BOOKS CAN BE TWENTY-FOUR, THIRTY-SIX, OR FORTY-EIGHT PAGES LONG, AND YOUR STORY SHOULD BE ABLE TO FIT INTO A COMIC OF ONE OF THESE LENGTHS. IT'S NO FUN TO GET TO THE LAST PAGE OF A COMIC YOU'VE SPENT A LOT OF TIME DRAWING ONLY TO DISCOVER THAT YOU NEED ROOM FOR ONE MORE PANEL! THE EASIEST WAY TO AVOID A PROBLEM LIKE THIS IS TO PLAN YOUR COMIC STORY OUT CAREFULLY.

THERE ARE THREE BASIC STEPS A COMIC GOES THROUGH BEFORE IT IS READY TO BE INKED: THE **THUMBNAIL**, THE **ROUGH BREAKDOWN**, AND THE **FINISHED PAGE**.

THE **THUMBNAIL** IS MORE OF A SHORTHAND NOTE TO YOURSELF THAN ANYTHING ELSE. THUMBNAILS ARE SMALL-SCALE SKETCHES OF EACH PAGE OF YOUR STORY. IN YOUR THUMBNAILS IT'S NOT NECESSARY TO MAKE PERFECT DRAWINGS, OR EVEN TO SPEND A LOT OF TIME ON THEM. USE THE THUMBNAILS TO FIGURE OUT WHAT AND HOW MUCH YOU NEED TO SHOW IN EACH PANEL, WHAT KIND OF PANELS YOU'LL NEED TO USE, AND HOW MANY PAGES YOUR STORY WILL CALL FOR. A COMIC BOOK STORY SHOULD NOT END ON A HALF PAGE IF IT CAN BE HELPED - IT LOOKS SLOPPY AND UNFINISHED.

MOVE THINGS AROUND, PLAY WITH THE COMPOSITION AND THE PANELS UNTIL YOU ARE HAPPY WITH THE LOOK OF THE PAGES. MAKE THE STORY AS GOOD AND INTERESTING AS YOU ARE ABLE. IT'S MUCH EASIER TO CHANGE YOUR MIND ABOUT THE DRAWINGS HERE IN THE THUMBNAILS THAN IT WOULD BE LATER ON A FINISHED PAGE!

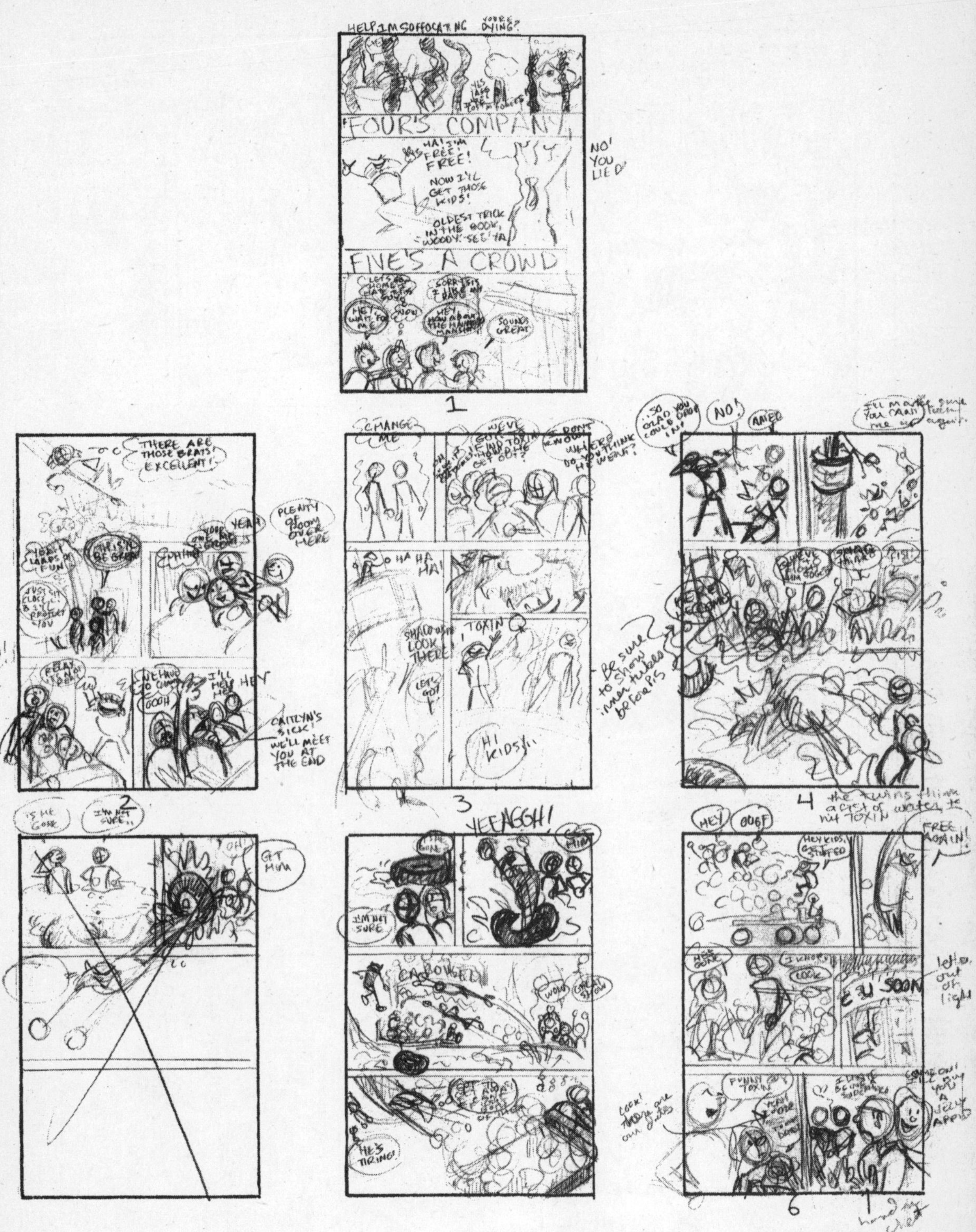

THIS IS A REDUCED COPY OF THE **THUMBNAILS** DONE FOR **SHADOWSTARS**. LOOK THESE SAMPLES OVER CAREFULLY AND COMPARE THEM TO THE ACTUAL PAGES IN THE COMIC BOOK TO SEE HOW THEY CHANGED FROM STEP TO STEP.

GWENN MERCADOCASIO "HOW TO DRAW DOMICS" PAGE# 1

REDUCED COPY OF THE **ROUGH** FOR PAGE ONE OF **SHADOWSTARS.**

GM
COMICS
S'HADOW
S'TARS'
TROUBLE
WITH
TOXIN
INSIDE!

HELD PRISONER UNDER GROUND, TOXIN ATTEMPTS HIS ESCAPE.
YOU'RE DYING?
I'M SUFFOCATING! I'VE LOST MY POWERS - THEY'RE GONE!
I'LL BRING YOU UP.
HURRY I'M CHOKING
FOUR'S COMPANY
HA!HA! I'M FREE!
NOW I CAN GET EVEN WITH SHADOWSIDE AND DAYSTAR FOR LOCKING ME UP!
YOU LIED!
SURE I LIED WOODY! ...OLDEST TRICK IN THE BOOK! SEE YOU!
FIVE'S A CROWD
HAUNTED MANSION
ARCADE
WAIT FOR ME CAITLYN!
JEREMY, LET'S GO HOME. I CAN'T STAND THIS GUY!
SORRY, SIS, I LIKE MY DATE.
HEY! LET'S GO IN THE HAUNTED MANSION!
SOUNDS GREAT.

AH! THERE ARE THOSE **BRATS** NOW! WAIT TILL THEY SEE ME AGAIN.

HAUNTED
MANSION
HORROR
JUST STAY WITH **ME** CAIT-LYN, **I'LL** PRO-TECT YOU.
THIS'LL BE **GREAT**
oh goody.

YOU **OWE** ME FOR THIS, **JEREMY**
UH HUH.
THERE'S **PLENTY** OF ROOM OVER HERE, **CAIT-LYN.**

IN A DARK PART OF THE TUNNEL, CAITLYN AND JEREMY BECOME DAYSTAR AND SHADOWSIDE.
WE'VE GOT TO FIND TOXIN! HOW DO YOU SUPPOSE HE GOT OUT.
I DON'T KNOW, BUT WE'VE GOT TO LOCK HIM BACK UP!

HA!HA!HA!HA!HA!HA!HA!HA!HA!HA!HA!HA!HA!HA!
OF FE
DAYSTAR! LOOK UP THERE!
LET'S GO!

HI, KIDS! REMEMBER ME?...
TOXIN!
ER

...SO GLAD YOU COULD DROP IN!
NO!
AIEE!

R OF FE
I'LL MAKE SURE YOU CAN'T LOCK ME UP AGAIN!
CAROUSEL

OOAF!
QUICK! TOXIN'S COMING!

SHADOWSIDE AND DAYSTAR MELD THEIR POWERS...
A FIST... A FIST...A FIST... A FIST... A FIST... A FIST...

ITS WORKING, SHADOWSIDE!

IS HE GONE?
I'M NOT SURE DAYSTAR.
LOOK AT THE COSTUMES.
SHADOWSIDE! LOOK OUT!
TOXIN'S BACK!
AFTER HIM!
HA! HA! HA! NO FAIR TWO AGAINST ONE!
WOW!
I DIDN'T KNOW THEY HAD SHOWS HERE.
THIS IS GREAT!

OUF!
HEY KIDS... GET STUFFED!
HEY!

YES! FREE AGAIN!

WE LOST HIM?
MMN HMN.

OH, WELL.
HEY, AREN'T THOSE OUR DATES?
WHERE?

SHE TOLD ME THAT SHE HATED THAT GUY!
DON'T WORRY! SHE WILL!

I HATE BEING A SUPERHERO.
COME ON! I'LL BUY YOU A JELLY APPLE.

ONCE YOU ARE HAPPY WITH YOUR THUMBNAILS IT'S TIME TO GO ON TO THE **ROUGHS**. THE **ROUGH BREAKDOWN** IS A FULL SIZED COMICS PAGE (11" X 17") AND IS WHERE YOU CAN BEGIN TO SPEND TIME ON YOUR DRAWINGS, BUT STILL HAVE THE LUXURY OF CHANGING YOUR MIND ABOUT THEM IF YOU WANT TO. AT THIS POINT IT IS A GOOD IDEA TO SKETCH IN ANY BALLOONS OR CAPTIONS, SO THAT YOU ARE SURE TO HAVE ENOUGH SPACE FOR THEM ON YOUR FINISHED PAGE.

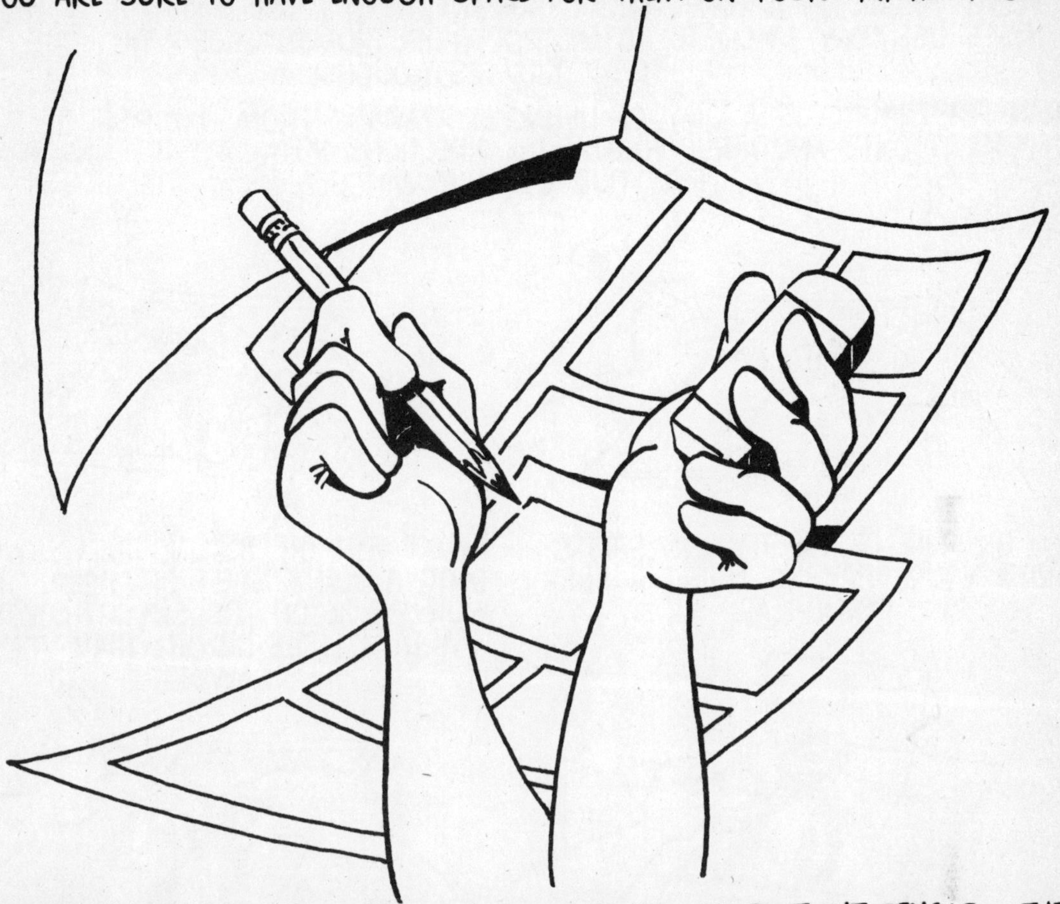

THE **FINISHED PAGE** IS WHERE YOU WILL DO WHAT IS CALLED **TIGHT PENCILS**. THESE ARE CLEAN, FINISHED DRAWINGS THAT SHOULD BE EASY FOR AN INKER TO READ AND WORK ON. IF YOU PLAN TO INK YOUR OWN COMICS THIS IS STILL NECESSARY. DIRTY OR PENCIL-SMEARED PAGES DON'T REPRODUCE WELL. IN FACT, THE DIRT USUALLY TENDS TO PRINT BETTER THAN THE ARTWORK!

IT MAY SEEM THAT YOU ARE DRAWING THE SAME ARTWORK OVER AND OVER, AND YOU ARE. THE IDEA IS THAT EACH VERSION OF YOUR STORY WILL GET BETTER AND SHARPER THAN THE LAST. SOME PEOPLE ARE ABLE TO SKIP A STEP WHEN THEY PLAN A COMIC BOOK, AND YOU MAY BE ONE OF THEM, BUT UNTIL YOU HAVE TRIED TO GO THROUGH ALL THREE STEPS AT LEAST ONCE, I WOULDN'T COUNT ON IT!

THERE ARE A FEW SHORTCUTS THAT CAN BE USED TO SPEED UP THE PROCESS INVOLVED IN TAKING A COMIC FROM THUMBNAILS TO FINISHED PAGES. A LOT OF ARTISTS USE **COPY-MACHINES** TO ENLARGE THEIR THUMBNAILS SO THAT THEY CAN RE-DRAW THEM AS ROUGHS.

TRANSFER TRACING IS A WAY OF LIFTING A DRAWING FROM ONE PIECE OF PAPER TO PLACE IT ONTO ANOTHER. FOLLOW THE DIRECTIONS BELOW TO TRY AND TRANSFER YOUR OWN DRAWINGS.

ON ONE SIDE OF THE TRACING PAPER, TRACE YOUR DRAWING USING A SOFT PENCIL-LEAD.

NEXT FLIP THE TRACING PAPER OVER ONTO A BLANK SHEET OF PAPER. RUB YOUR PENCIL ON IT'S SIDE TO COVER AN AREA A LITTLE LARGER THAN YOUR DRAWING.

FLIP THE TRACING PAPER BACK OVER AND POSITION THE DRAWING WHERE YOU WOULD LIKE IT. YOU MIGHT WANT TO USE REMOVABLE TAPE TO HOLD IT IN PLACE.

NOW TRACE THE DRAWING AGAIN USING A HARD PENCIL-LEAD. BE CAREFUL NOT TO PRESS TOO HARD AND TEAR THE PAPER!

WHEN YOU ARE DONE TRACING, LIFT THE PAPER AND YOU WILL FIND YOUR DRAWING THERE!

ANOTHER WAY OF COPYING A DRAWING FROM ONE PAGE TO ANOTHER IS TO USE A **LIGHT-BOX**. THIS IS PROBABLY THE CLEANEST WAY TO WORK, BUT HARD ON THE EYES. A LIGHT SHINES THROUGH THE BOTTOM OF A PLEXIGLASS TABLE SO THAT WHEN YOU PLACE A CLEAN COMICS PAGE OVER YOUR DRAWINGS THEY SHOW THROUGH THE PAGE SO THAT THEY CAN BE TRACED OVER. A LIGHT-BOX IS NOT VERY COMPLICATED TO BUILD AND IS AN INVALUABLE TOOL.

TOOLS

COMICS CAN BE DRAWN ON ALMOST ANYTHING. MOST ARTISTS USE **2-PLY BRISTOL PAPER**, BUT BRISTOL BOARD, PLATE BRISTOL, AND EVEN TRACING PAPER OR ACETATE MAY BE USED. TRY A FEW INEXPENSIVE BRANDS TO SEE WHICH KIND YOU LIKE BEST BEFORE SPENDING A LOT OF MONEY ON PAPER.

COMIC PAGES ARE DRAWN IN PENCIL BEFORE THEY ARE INKED. A LOT OF ARTISTS USE **NON-REPRO BLUE PENCILS** TO DO THEIR DRAWINGS. THESE ARE PENCILS THAT DON'T HAVE ENOUGH BLACK OR RED PIGMENT IN THEM TO BE SEEN BY THE CAMERAS USED TO REPRODUCE ARTWORK. WHEN YOU USE NON-REPRO BLUE PENCIL IT IS NOT NECESSARY TO ERASE THE PENCIL AFTER INKING. IF YOU ARE USING REGULAR PENCILS, BE SURE TO KEEP THE PENCIL-LINE LIGHT SO THEY WON'T BE TOO HARD TO ERASE LATER. **2-B PENCILS** ARE MY FAVORITE BECAUSE THEY ARE SO SOFT, AND YOU DON'T HAVE TO PRESS VERY HARD TO GET A GOOD PENCIL-LINE WITH THEM. YOU MAY FIND THAT YOU LIKE HARDER PENCIL LEADS. TRY A FEW TYPES SO YOU'LL KNOW WHAT KIND IS BEST FOR YOU.

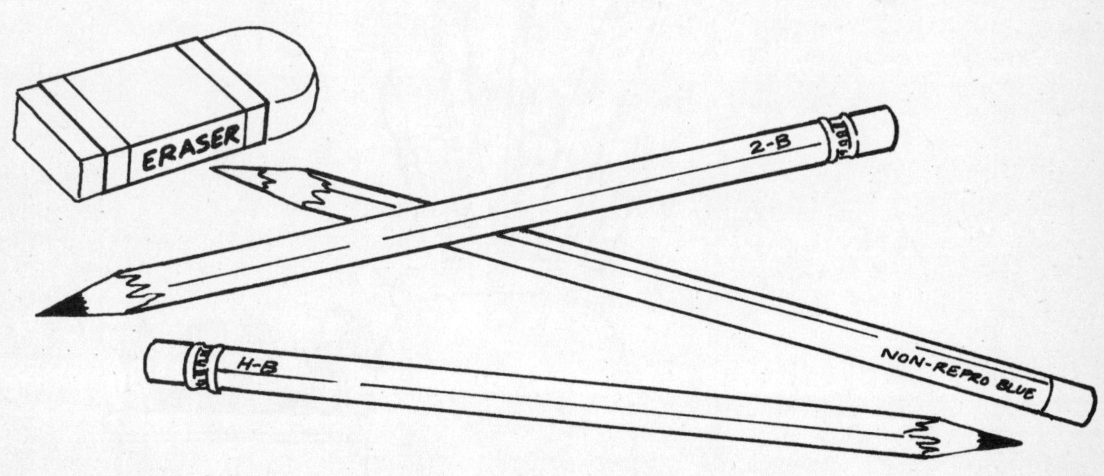

YOU WILL ALSO WANT TO GET A SEPARATE ERASER. THE PINK ERASERS THAT ARE ATTACHED TO COMMON PENCILS CAN SMEAR OR EVEN TEAR YOUR PAPER IF YOU PRESS TO HARD WITH THEM.

YOU WILL NEED TO **RULE** THE BORDERS AND OTHER PARTS OF YOUR COMIC PAGES. A **CLEAR TRIANGLE WITH A RULED SIDE** IS A GREAT TOOL, BUT YOU CAN USE A RULER AS WELL. AN EIGHTEEN INCH RULER WILL BE BIG ENOUGH TO RULE THE LENGTH OF YOUR PAGE WITHOUT HAVING TO MOVE IT AROUND.

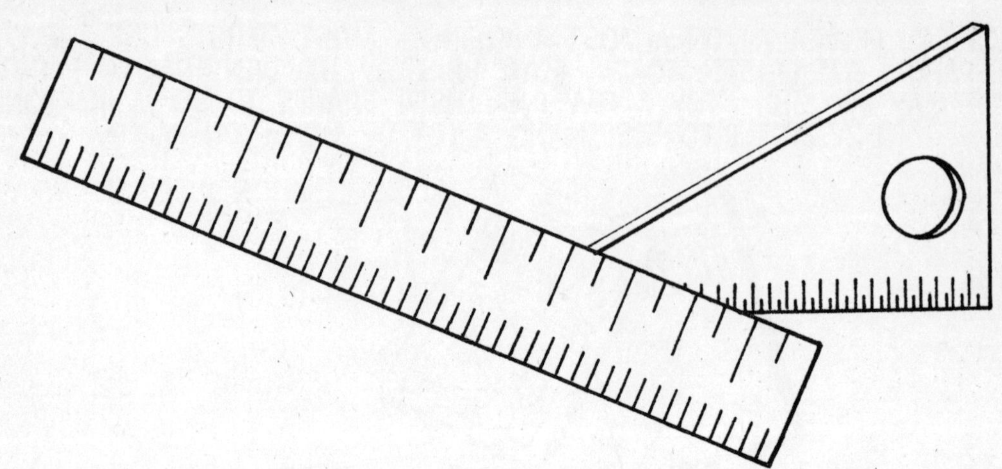

THERE ARE A LOT OF OTHER TOOLS THAT YOU MAY WANT TO PICK UP AS YOU GO ALONG, OR LATER ON WHEN YOUR SKILLS ARE MORE ADVANCED. AT THE END OF THIS BOOK YOU WILL FIND A LIST OF THOSE MATERIALS. THEY ARE NOT INCLUDED HERE BECAUSE WHEN YOU ARE FIRST STARTING TO DRAW COMICS YOU SHOULD CONCENTRATE ON GETTING AS GOOD AS YOU CAN AT THE DRAWING AND STORYTELLING.

I KNOW IT SOUNDS DULL, BUT IT'S TRUE; YOU SHOULD LEARN TO BUILD A HOUSE BEFORE YOU TRY TO PUT A ROOF ON IT!

ANATOMY FOR COMICS

IN THIS BOOK WE ARE CONCENTRATING ON DRAWING ACCURATE FIGURES FOR COMIC BOOKS, AND THERE ARE ABOUT A BIZILLION DIFFERENT WAYS TO START. THE TWO SYSTEMS I LIKE BEST ARE **MEASURING** AND **BUILDING** THE FIGURE WITH SHAPES.

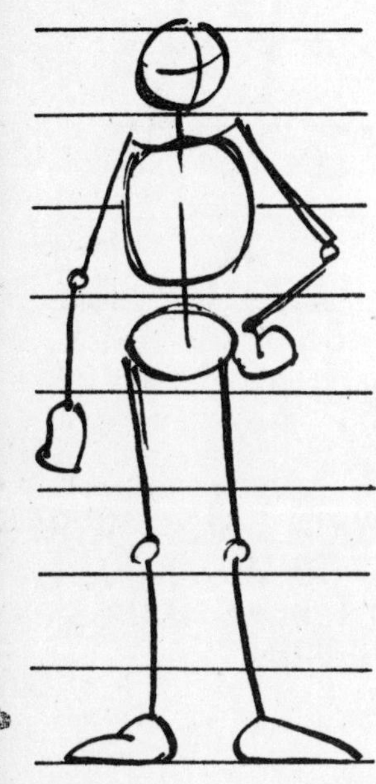

WHEN YOU USE THE **MEASURING SYSTEM**, YOU DIVIDE THE BODY INTO EIGHT PARTS, EACH PART EQUAL TO THE SIZE OF ONE HEAD, THAT WHEN PUT TOGETHER MAKE UP A PERFECTLY PROPORTIONED FIGURE.

WHEN YOU **BUILD A FIGURE**, YOU PUT SHAPES TOGETHER, PLACING A CIRCLE ON TOP OF A BEAN-SHAPE AND SO ON, UNTIL YOU'VE GOT A RECOGNIZABLE FIGURE.

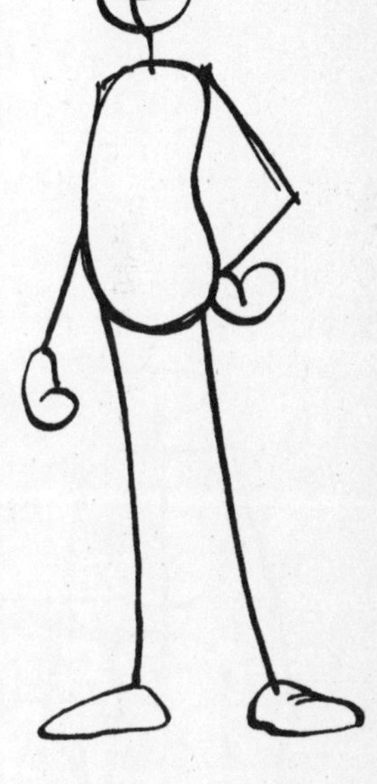

THESE SYSTEMS ARE NOT MEANT TO TEACH YOU TO DRAW IN ANY PARTICULAR STYLE. ANY SYSTEM IS JUST A SHORTCUT METHOD OF GETTING TO THE ACTUAL DRAWING, AND ONCE YOU MASTER ONE OR MORE OF THEM, YOU'LL DEVELOP YOUR OWN SYSTEM AND STYLE.

THERE IS REALLY NO EXCUSE FOR DRAWING BAD FIGURES...YOU TAKE YOUR OWN EVERYWHERE YOU GO, SO LOOK AT IT! LOOK IN THE MIRROR, STUDY PHOTOGRAPHS FROM MAGAZINES, WATCH THE PEOPLE AROUND YOU EVERY DAY. STUDY THE FIGURE UNTIL YOU KNOW IT. THINK ABOUT HOW YOUR ARM FITS WITH YOUR SHOULDER, OR HOW LONG YOUR LEG IS COMPARED TO THE REST OF YOUR BODY.

THE NEXT THREE PAGES IS A LIST OF MEASUREMENTS THAT YOU CAN USE TO CHECK YOUR DRAWINGS TO SEE IF THE PROPORTIONS ARE RIGHT.

EIGHT HEADS EQUAL ONE AVERAGE BODY. NINE OR TEN HEADS EQUALS ONE SUPERHUMAN BODY.

EIGHT HEADS EQUALS MEN. SEVEN AND A HALF EQUALS WOMEN. FOUR TO FIVE HEADS EQUALS CHILDREN.

CHILDREN'S HEADS APPEAR LARGER IN RELATION TO THEIR BODIES THAN ADULT HEADS APPEAR TO THEIRS.

WHEN YOU SPREAD THE FINGERS ON YOUR HAND, IT WILL JUST ABOUT COVER YOUR FACE.

IF YOU BEND YOUR ARM IN HALF, THE UPPER ARM IS SLIGHTLY SHORTER THAN THE LOWER ARM INCLUDING YOUR HAND.

YOUR ELBOW MEETS YOUR WAIST JUST ABOVE YOUR HIP.

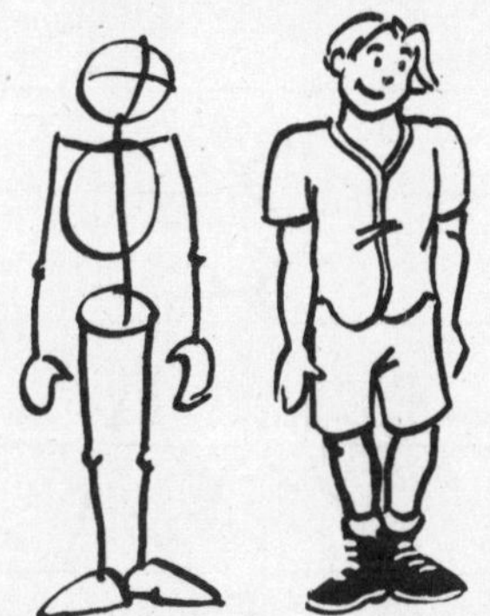

WHEN YOU ALLOW YOUR ARM TO HANG AT YOUR SIDE, THE TIPS OF YOUR FINGERS WILL STOP AT MID-THIGH.

IF YOU START AT THE WRIST, APPROXIMATELY THREE HANDS EQUAL ONE ARM.

TWO HEADS EQUAL THE UPPER LEG. TWO HEADS EQUAL THE LOWER LEG AND FOOT TOGETHER.

OF COURSE, NO TWO FIGURES ARE EXACTLY ALIKE. THERE ARE SHORT-WAISTED PEOPLE AND LONG-LEGGED PEOPLE, THERE ARE TINY PEOPLE AND HUGE PEOPLE. ALL A DRAWING SYSTEM CAN DO FOR YOU IS GIVE YOU A BASIC FIGURE TO START WITH. YOU'VE GOT TO PRACTICE AND EXPERIMENT WITH ALL OF THE DIFFERENT BODY TYPES UNTIL YOU'VE GOT THEM RIGHT!

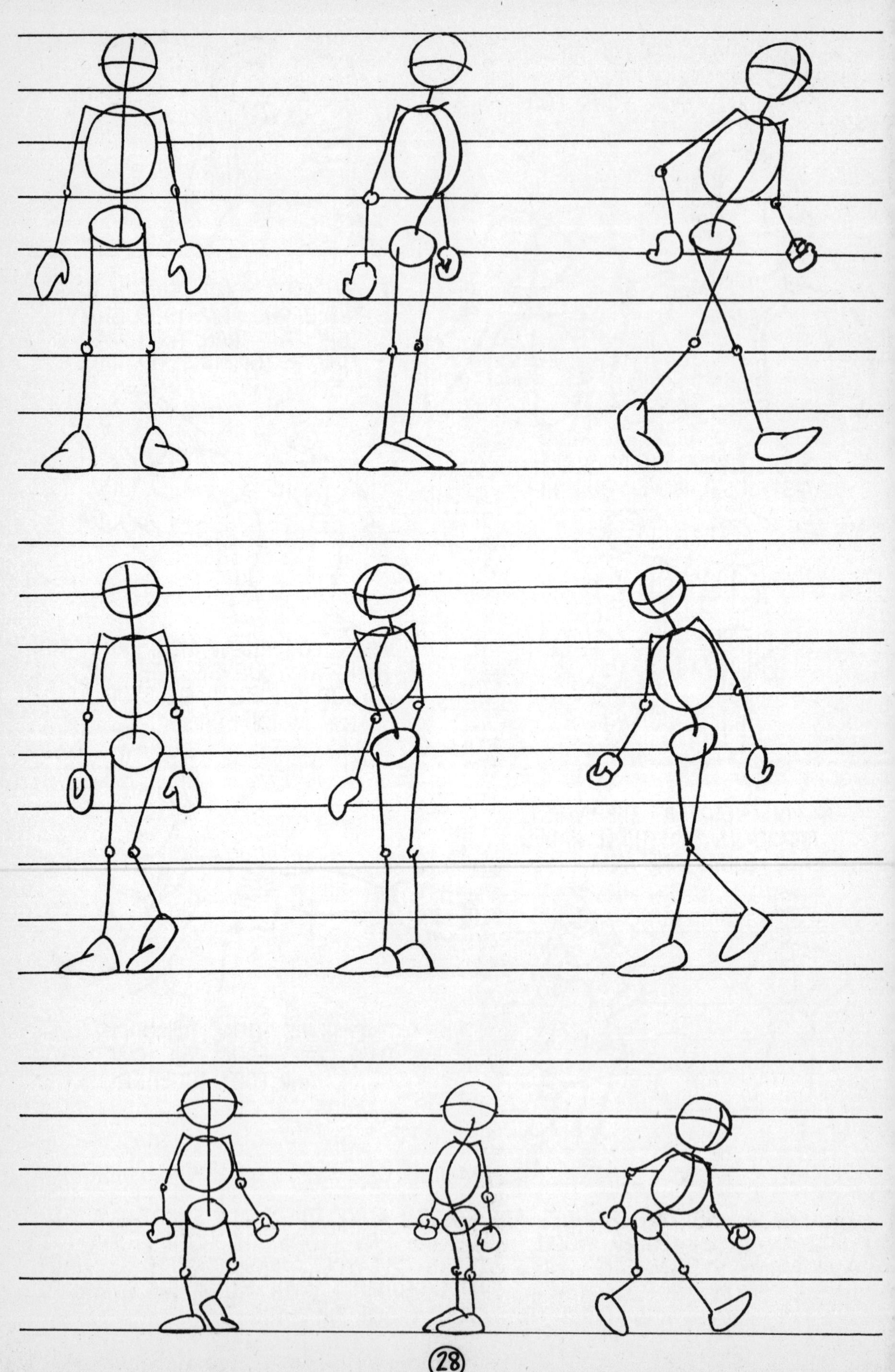

THE SAMPLE FIGURES IN THESE DRAWING SYSTEMS ARE NOT COMPLETE FIGURES, IN FACT THEY LOOK MORE LIKE SKELETONS OR STICK FIGURES THAN ANYTHING ELSE RIGHT NOW! PRACTICE WITH THESE SIMPLE FIGURES BEFORE YOU TRY ADDING MASS TO THE BODY, OR START FUSSING WITH FACES. WHEN YOU CAN DRAW AN ACCURATE FIGURE NINE TIMES OUT OF TEN, AND MAKE IT RUN, JUMP, AND FLY, THEN YOU CAN GO ON TO THE NEXT PART OF THIS CHAPTER.

TO **ADD MASS** TO THE FIGURE, WE ARE GOING TO ADD SHAPES TO OUR SKELETONS. USING BALLS AND OVALS, WE WILL ADD ON THE MUSCLES, THEN "COVER THEM WITH SKIN" BY OUTLINING. DON'T OUTLINE EVERY BUMP! SMOOTH OUT YOUR LINE AS YOU GO AND WITH PRACTICE YOUR FIGURES WILL START TO LOOK MORE REALISTIC.

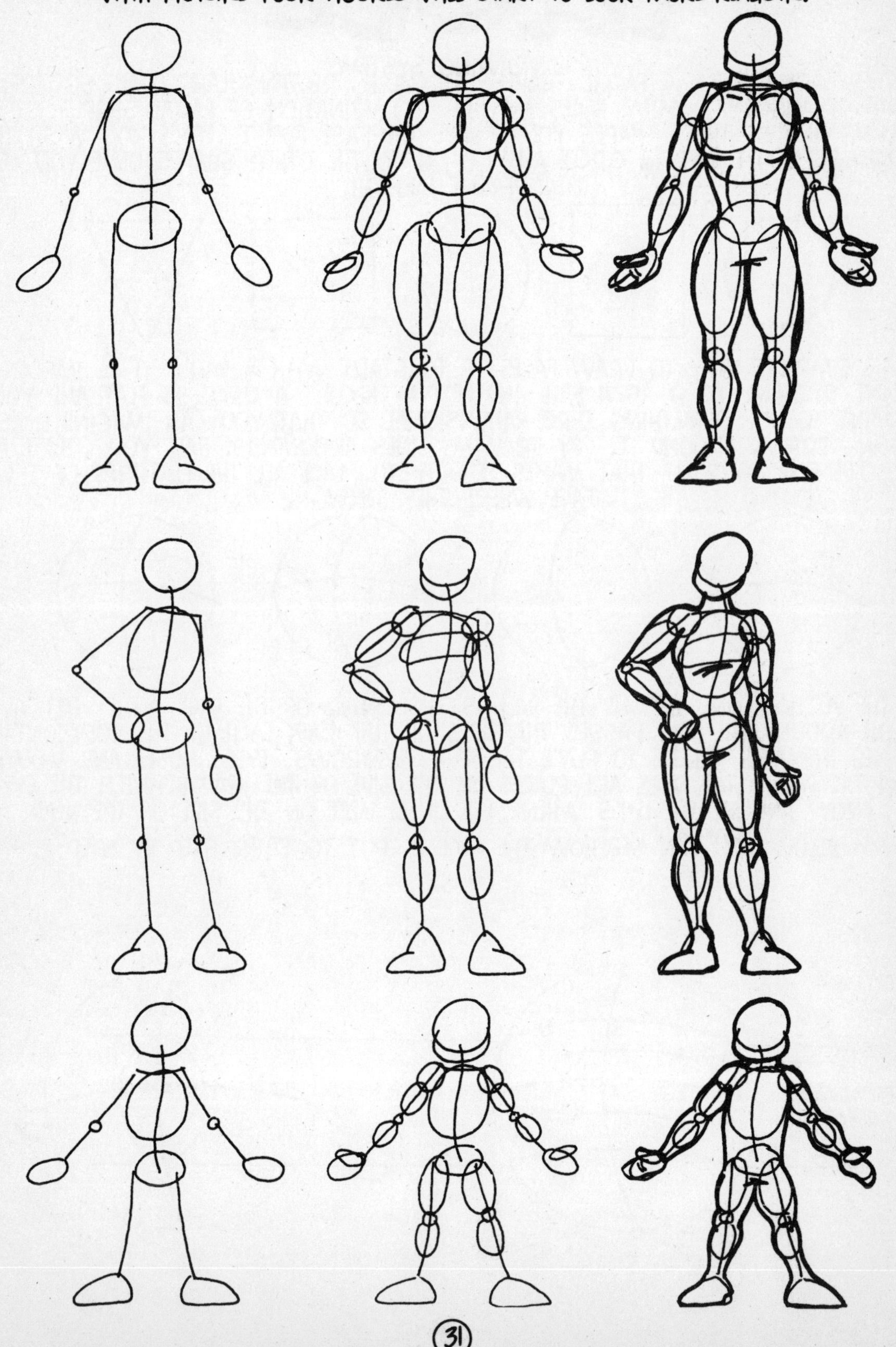

THERE ARE FIVE BASIC FACIAL SHAPES: CIRCULAR, RECTANGULAR, OVAL, SQUARE, AND TRIANGULAR. SOME FACES MAY BE A COMBINATION OF FACIAL SHAPES. BY USING ANY OF THESE SHAPES YOU'LL HAVE THE BASE FOR THE FACE YOU WISH TO DRAW. START WITH A CIRCLE AND GO ON TO THE OTHER SHAPES ONCE YOU FEEL CONFIDENT ENOUGH.

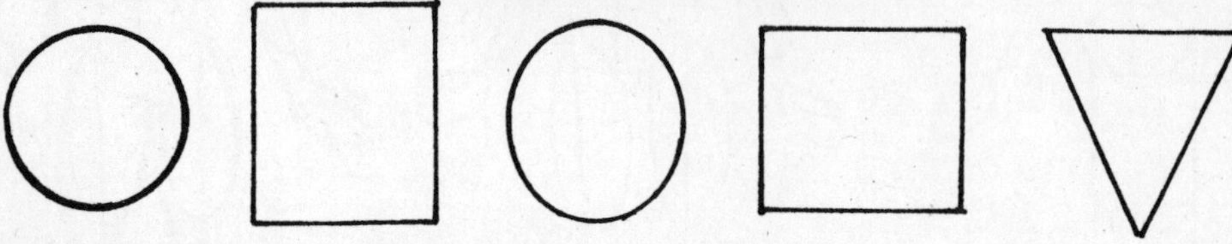

THE SIMPLEST WAY TO DRAW FACES IS TO START WITH A BALL. IT IS IMPORTANT TO THINK OF IT AS A BALL AND NOT A CIRCLE. A CIRCLE IS FLAT AND YOU WANT TO USE SOMETHING **THREE-DIMENSIONAL** SO THAT YOU CAN IMAGINE LINES BEING DRAWN AROUND IT. BY DRAWING LINES AROUND THE BALL YOU CREATE A GUIDE FOR YOURSELF THAT MAKES IT EASY TO PLACE ALL THE FEATURES OF THE FACE WHERE THEY BELONG.

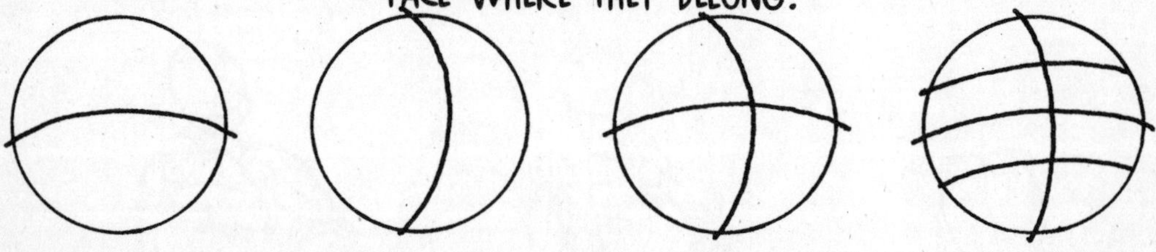

THE VERTICAL LINE AROUND THE BALL IS THE CENTER OF THE FACE. THE VERTICAL LINE AROUND THE BALL PASSES THE SIDES OF THE HEAD. EACH OF THE HORIZONTAL LINES INDICATES WHERE TO PLACE THE HAIR, EYEBROWS, EYES, NOSE, AND MOUTH ON THE FACE. THE EARS ARE PLACED ON THE SIDE OF THE HEAD BETWEEN THE EYEBROW AND MOUTH LINES WHERE THE LINES MEET ON THE SIDE OF THE HEAD.

BELOW YOU CAN SEE HOW THE FACE IS PUT TOGETHER STEP BY STEP.

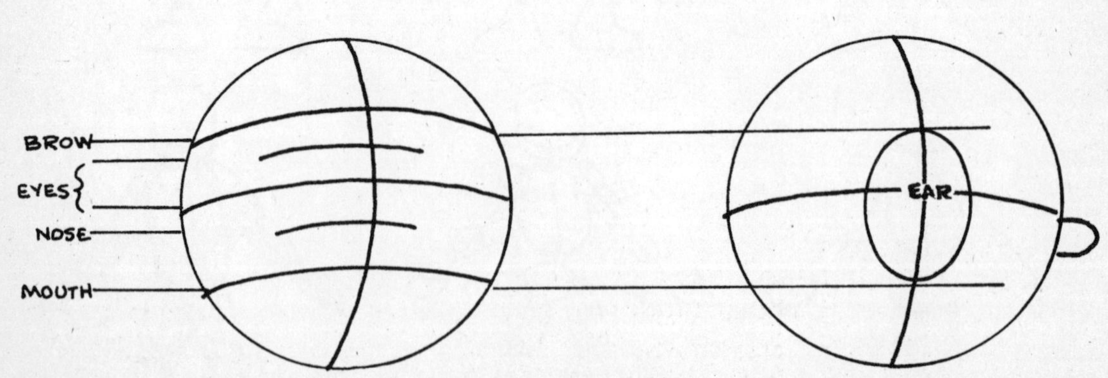

BY ADDING SHAPES, A SMALL SQUARE FOR THE CHIN, OR CIRCLES FOR CHEEKS YOU CAN MAKE THE FACE MORE COMPLICATED. HERE ARE SOME EXAMPLES:

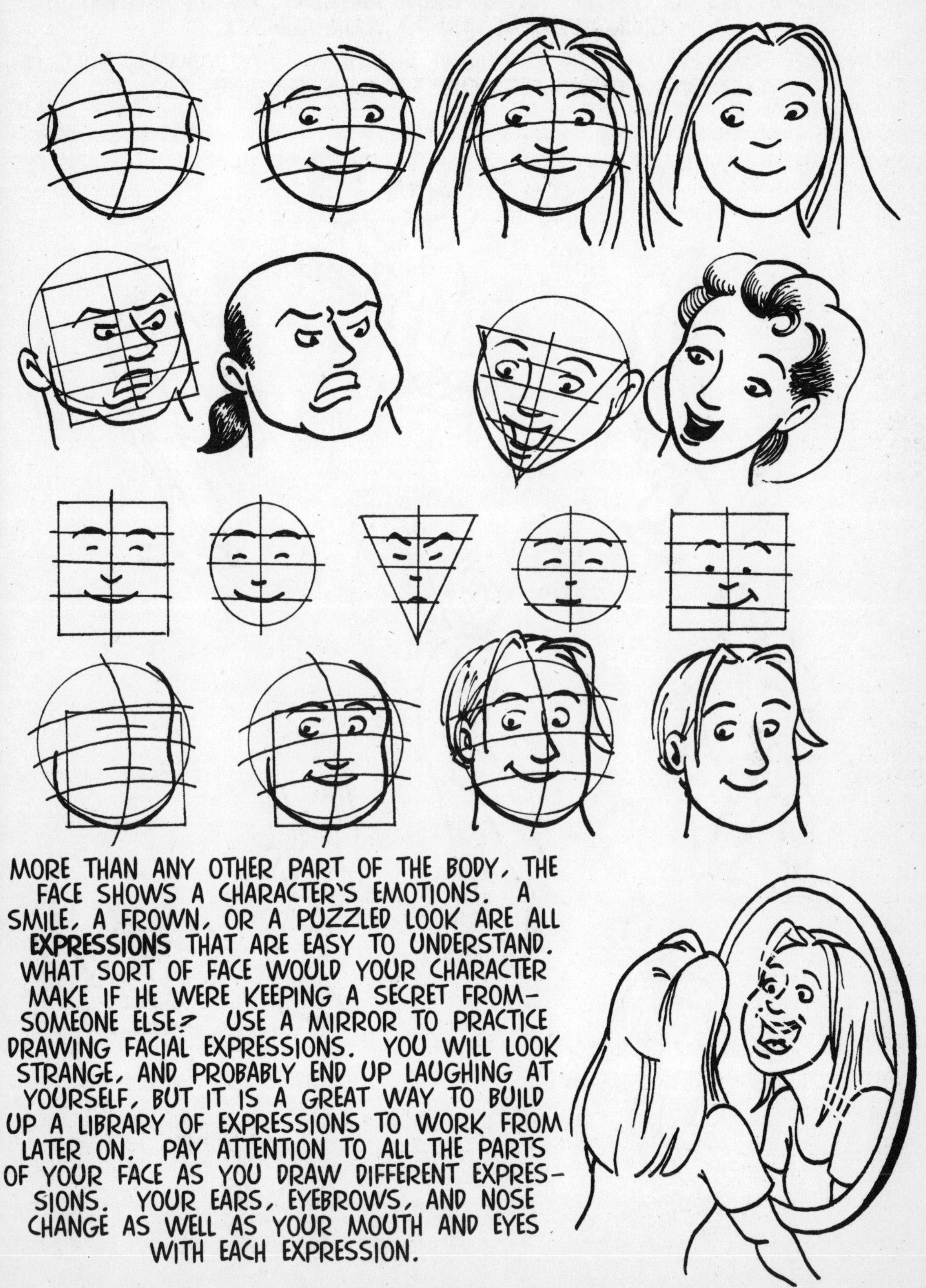

MORE THAN ANY OTHER PART OF THE BODY, THE FACE SHOWS A CHARACTER'S EMOTIONS. A SMILE, A FROWN, OR A PUZZLED LOOK ARE ALL **EXPRESSIONS** THAT ARE EASY TO UNDERSTAND. WHAT SORT OF FACE WOULD YOUR CHARACTER MAKE IF HE WERE KEEPING A SECRET FROM SOMEONE ELSE? USE A MIRROR TO PRACTICE DRAWING FACIAL EXPRESSIONS. YOU WILL LOOK STRANGE, AND PROBABLY END UP LAUGHING AT YOURSELF, BUT IT IS A GREAT WAY TO BUILD UP A LIBRARY OF EXPRESSIONS TO WORK FROM LATER ON. PAY ATTENTION TO ALL THE PARTS OF YOUR FACE AS YOU DRAW DIFFERENT EXPRESSIONS. YOUR EARS, EYEBROWS, AND NOSE CHANGE AS WELL AS YOUR MOUTH AND EYES WITH EACH EXPRESSION.

A CHARACTER MAY ALSO EXPRESS EMOTIONS THROUGH HIS BODY LANGUAGE. WHEN A CHARACTER THAT USUALLY STANDS ERECT IS SHOWN SLOUCHED OVER WITH HIS ARMS HANGING LIMP AT HIS SIDES, WE UNDERSTAND THE EMOTION BEING EXPRESSED BY HIS BODY. THIS IS **EXPRESSIVE ANATOMY**, AND IS ANOTHER WAY OF GIVING INFORMATION TO YOUR AUDIENCE.

BELOW ARE SOME EXAMPLES OF EXPRESSIVE ANATOMY. TRY DRAWING SOME OF YOUR OWN FIGURES SHOWING THE SAME EMOTIONS TOO.

CHARACTER DESIGN

WHEN I DESIGN A CHARACTER, I USUALLY SELECT THE CHARACTER'S OUTSTANDING PERSONALITY TRAIT AND TRY TO MAKE THAT SHOW IN THE WAY THAT CHARACTER LOOKS. FOR EXAMPLE, **SHADOWSIDE** AND **DAYSTAR** DON'T WANT ANYONE TO KNOW WHO THEY ARE WHEN THEY ASSUME THEIR SUPERHERO IDENTITIES, SO THEY WEAR MASKS THAT COVER MOST OF THEIR FACES. THEY ARE BOTH TEENAGERS, SO I TRIED NOT TO MAKE THEM TOO HUGE AND FULL OF MUSCLES WHEN THEY ARE IN COSTUME, SINCE IN "REAL LIFE" THEY ARE STILL GROWING AND HAVEN'T REACHED THEIR FULL SIZE YET.

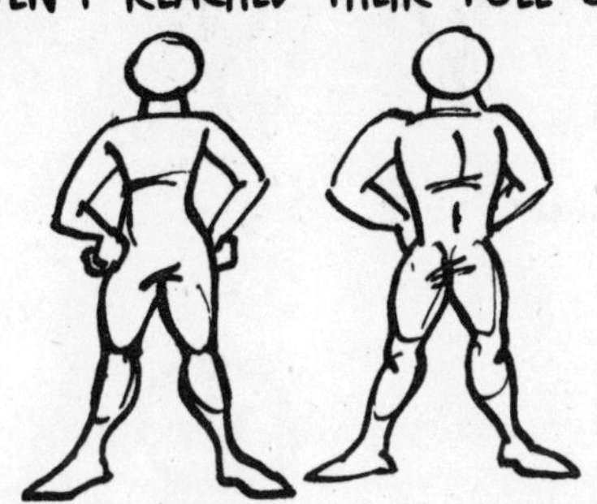

I WANTED TO SHOW HOW EVIL **TOXIN** IS BY MAKING HIM UGLY. THIS IS A SIMPLE, STEREOTYPICAL WAY TO MAKE IT OBVIOUS TO THE AUDIENCE THAT **TOXIN** IS THE BAD GUY, BUT IT DOES WORK. **TOXIN** ALSO DOES NOT WEAR A MASK BECAUSE HE DOESN'T CARE WHO SEES HIM SINCE HE THINKS OF HIMSELF AS THE MOST POWERFUL BEING ALIVE.

IF YOU WANT TO USE STEREOTYPES, THEN YOUR GOOD GUYS WILL BE LARGER THAN LIFE-SIZED AND GOOD LOOKING. THE BAD GUYS WILL BE EXAGGERATED IN SIZE, AND UGLY.

REMEMBER THOUGH, THAT THE MORE YOU GO AGAINST STEREOTYPES, THE MORE INTERESTING YOUR CHARACTERS WILL BE. WHAT IF YOU CREATED A SUPERHERO THAT WAS CROSS-EYED OR A VILLAIN THAT LOOKED LIKE AN INFANT?

HERE ARE SOME CHARACTER TYPES FOR YOU TO USE AS MODELS.

NOW IT'S TIME FOR YOU TO DESIGN YOUR OWN CHARACTERS! REMEMBER THAT ANY KIND OF CHARACTER CAN BE IN A COMIC BOOK...YOU CAN DRAW YOURSELF AS A CHARACTER IN YOUR COMICS IF YOU WANT TO!

CONCLUSION

REMEMBER THAT IT TAKES A LOT OF TIME AND PRACTICE TO BE GOOD AT ANYTHING, AND IT TAKES REAL DETERMINATION TO BE GREAT. THE PEOPLE WHO DRAW THE COMIC BOOKS YOU LIKE BEST HAVE BEEN STUDYING AND WORKING AT IT FOR YEARS TO GET AS GOOD AS THEY ARE NOW, SO DON'T GIVE UP IF YOUR DRAWINGS DON'T LOOK EXACTLY THE WAY YOU WANT THEM TO AT FIRST. KEEP PRACTICING!

EXERCISES

THIS IS A LIST OF EXERCISES YOU CAN DO TO HELP IMPROVE YOUR SKILLS FOR DRAWING COMIC BOOKS. IT'S INTERESTING TO DO THEM MORE THAN ONCE, A FEW WEEKS APART TO SEE THE DIFFERENT WAYS YOU WILL DRAW THEM AS YOUR SKILLS IMPROVE. ALWAYS DATE YOUR WORK SO THAT YOU'LL SEE THE PROGRESS YOU MAKE FROM YOUR EARLY COMICS TO THE PRESENT.

1. RULE YOUR PAPER WITH NINE HORIZONTAL LINES SO THAT IT IS DIVIDED INTO EIGHT EQUAL SPACES. DRAW THREE FIGURES EACH OF A MAN, A WOMAN AND A CHILD IN DIFFERENT POSES.

2. DRAW A FIGURE IN EACH OF THE FOLLOWING POSES: KNEELING, RUNNING, SEATED, STRETCHING, TWISTING, FLYING, AND THROWING A BALL.

3. DRAW A FIGURE FOR EACH OF THE FOLLOWING SO THAT THE WAY THE FIGURE FEELS IS OBVIOUS: ANGER, FEAR, SADNESS, LOVE, HATE, SHYNESS, AND SLEEPINESS.

4. DRAW A FACE FOR EACH OF THE FIVE BASIC FACIAL SHAPES: TRIANGULAR, RECTANGULAR, OVAL, CIRCULAR, AND SQUARE.

5. FOR EACH OF THE FOLLOWING EXAMPLES USE THREE PANELS EACH TO SHOW: A CAR CHASE, WATER DRIPPING FROM A FAUCET, A PERSON DISCOVERING THAT THEY HAVE JUST WON THE LOTTERY.

6. FOR EACH OF THE FOLLOWING EXAMPLES, CHOOSE A CAMERA ANGLE THAT YOU THINK BEST SHOWS THE INFORMATION IN THE PANEL. USE ONLY ONE PANEL FOR EACH. SOMEONE WHO IS ABOUT TO BE ATTACKED, TWO FRIENDS SEARCHING FOR EACH OTHER IN A CROWD, SOMEONE HITTING A HOMERUN, AND SOMEONE KEEPING A SECRET.

IT IS ALSO AN EXCELLENT IDEA TO KEEP A SKETCHBOOK WITH YOU AT ALL TIMES. THIS WAY YOU CAN DRAW WHENEVER YOU WANT TO, OR YOU CAN SKETCH OUT YOUR IDEAS BEFORE YOU FORGET THEM. TRY TO DRAW AS MANY DIFFERENT KINDS OF THINGS AS YOU CAN. THINK OF YOUR SKETCHBOOK AS A DIARY OF PICTURES. DRAW AS MUCH AS YOU CAN EVERY DAY. PRACTICE. PRACTICE! **PRACTICE!**

BELOW IS A LIST OF MATERIALS YOU MIGHT WANT TO PURCHASE AS YOUR SKILLS IMPROVE. BE CAREFUL TO BUY ONLY WHAT YOU NEED; IT'S VERY EASY TO SPEND A SMALL FORTUNE ON ART SUPPLIES ONCE YOU ARE IN THE STORE. (I HAVE A COLLECTION OF NOT-SO-CHEAP SUPPLIES THAT I HAVEN'T EVEN USED, BUT THEY SEEMED SO INTERESTING IN THE STORE THAT I JUST HAD TO HAVE THEM!)

- A LETTERING GUIDE, FOR RULING SPEECH BALLOONS AND CAPTIONS.
- A PAD OR ROLL OF TRACING PAPER
- A BOUND SKETCHBOOK
- INDIA INK, AND THE PEN-NIBS AND HOLDER FOR THEM, FOR INKING COMICS.
- COLORED INKS
- NUMBER ONE AND TWO ROUND-POINT WATERCOLOR BRUSHES, FOR INKING COMICS.
- A LIGHT-BOX
- ARTISTS ANATOMY BOOKS, FOR REFERENCE
- BOOKS ON LETTERING STYLES AND TYPEFACES, FOR REFERENCE

I'M SURE THERE ARE A LOT MORE SUPPLIES I COULD LIST HERE, BUT THESE ARE BASICS. THOUGH THIS BOOK DID NOT DEAL WITH INKING AND COLORING, THE MATERIALS TO DO SO ARE ON THIS LIST. IF YOU FEEL YOU ARE READY START EXPERIMENTING WITH INKS AND COLOR, GET USED TO THE PENS AND BRUSHES. THIS WILL ONLY MAKE IT THAT MUCH EASIER FOR YOU TO DEVELOP THESE SKILLS ONCE THE OPPORTUNITY TO LEARN HOW TO USE THEM FORMALLY COMES ALONG.